A DREAM OF SPRINGTIME

A DREAM OF SPRINGTIME

Alicia Ostriker

THE SMITH
by arrangement with Horizon Press
New York 1979

design
by Alicia Ostriker

© Copyright 1979 by Alicia Ostriker
All rights reserved
First Edition
Library of Congress Catalog Number: 78-59769
ISBN: 0-912292-53-9

Published by THE SMITH
5 Beekman Street
NYC 10038

CONTENTS

I
ANNIE AND ME	7
BECKY AND BENNY IN FAR ROCKAWAY	9
TWO RELATIVES	10
SONNET. TO TELL THE TRUTH	11
AS FORESTS DEAD AND RESTING	12
OLD MEN	13
CLOTHING AND NOTHING	14
ANNIE, APHRODITE, AND THE ELEVATOR	15
THE LITTLE FRIEND	17
PER ASPERA AD ASTRA	18
LOVE & FOOD	19
COMMUNITAS	20

II
PORTRAITE D'ARTISTE	24
PORTRAIT OF A MAN	25
THE WOLVES	26
FIRE: A PARABLE	27
CAPE HATTERAS, EASTER WEEKEND	28
THE HILLS	30
SKATING	31
PROPERTY	32
THE INCOMPLEAT GARDNER	34
WINE	36
THE KILLING	37

III
THE FOOL STANDS UP TO TEACH *KING LEAR* AGAIN	39
NOON CONCERT	40
THE CLOCK ABOVE THE KITCHEN DOOR SAYS ONE	42
IN THE MUSEUM	43
THE COLLEAGUE	46
THIRST	47
MY LECTURE TO THE WRITING STUDENTS	48
NEW JERSEY SUNSET	50

IV
A DREAM OF SPRINGTIME	54
BLACK MEN, WHITE TEETH, BERKELEY CAMPUS	59
THE FREEWAY	60

© Copyright 1978 by Alicia Ostriker

ACKNOWLEDGEMENTS

The following poems have appeared in *Once More Out of Darkness, and other Poems* (Berkeley Poets' Co-op Press, 1974; reprinted 1976): Annie and Me, Sonnet to Tell the Truth, Old Men, Portraite d'Artiste and Ripping.

The following appeared in the collection *I Take my Real Body: Poems by Six Women* (Rutgers University Women's Studies Institute, 1976): Portraite d'Artiste, Communitas.

The following poems originally appeared or will appear in:
Carleton Miscellany: Andante, Berkshire Hills
Arts in Society: Cape Hatteras
Quarterly Review Of Literature: Wine, The Killing
New Orleans Review: The Clock Above the Kitchen Wall
American Poetry Review: A Dream of Springtime (conclusion)
Shenandoah: Thirst
US 1 Worksheets: Fire, In The Museum, New Jersey Sunset (this also appeared in *The Villager*), Becky and Benny, Per Aspera Ad Astra, The Fool Stands Up, My Lecture to the Writing Students.
The Third Thing: The Freeway
Berkeley Poets' Co-op: Annie & Me, Love & Food
Poetry Now: The Blood, Old Men (revised version)
Second Berkshire Anthology: The Wolves, Communitas
Four Zoas: Like an Orphan
Velvet Wings: Black Men, White Teeth
Minnesota Review: The Killing (revised version)
Rufus: Property
Momentum: Fire
California Quarterly: Becky and Benny (revised version).

for Rebecca, Eve and Gabriel

****

Do I contradict myself?
Very well then, I contradict myself.
I am large, I contain multitudes.

    Walt Whitman, grandmother of American poetry

I

*For we are put on earth a little space
That we may learn to bear the beams of love.*

William Blake

Annie and Me

Every truly beautiful girl needs a lump-type girl as a best friend
And the rules of their association are, one, they confide everything
                                                        to each other,
And, two, neither the beauty of the former, nor the lumphood of
                                                        the latter,
Shall be acknowledged verbally by either
And my mommy said everyone was just jealous
Because of my I.Q.
Or—what?
Only she grew, a daisy, in my building—Annie—

In Annie's apartment I was shocked by the arrangements.
Five of eight snottynose kids in a bed, everywhere Mary & Jesus
                                                        & saints
& knicknacks, behind the door hung a cat-o-nine-tails
I couldn't guess what it was until they told me
Nor could believe it used by Mister Hayward
That gentle alcoholic on relief—
Who walked me once to the subway and praised my posture—
Mister Hayward stood at that fifth floor window
And cried to his scolding wife and oldest daughters
"If you don't stop I'll jump!" They didn't stop, and he soared
Down to a spot in the hedged and wired garden.

My mommy, whose windows the Italian brothers broke
Again, because she hectored them not to play benchball *right* there

Said I could be popular
If I would remember to always be nice to people.
How could I? I hated people.
Annie got hips and bosoms early,
Many years ago we sat on the concrete stoop together in April,
I bet I sat like a slob, with my bloomers showing,
And I bet they were torn and dirty, and my socks had holes
I tried to tuck in my shoes
And that Annie in a see-thru blouse sat like a primrose.
"Do you know why I'm sorry my father died?" Silence.

"Who'll walk down the aisle with me now when I get married?"
O blush I ruby now for my gasp then.

My mommy read me books—I sat and drew—
The whole damned world played running away from me.
I would recall all this, old whelm, regurgitate.
Speak, memory, or I'll kick the shit out of you.

Becky and Benny in Far Rockaway

Near the Atlantic Ocean, past the last subway station,
Streaks of sand on the sidewalk,
Armies of aging Jews, soaking up sun
As if it were Talmud,
And the rickety white stairs
To an apartment like a frail body.

My uncle and aunt were both warty, like alligators.
They set a lunch on the oilcloth-covered table.
I felt peculiar about the smells.

The lunch seemed to go on all afternoon,
Anxious syllables fluttering over my head like fireflies.
Shayne Maydel was me.
Eat, they said in English, eat.
So I ate, and finally reached the pastoral scene,
Bo Peep, pink roses, green leaves
At the dish bottom,
One of those sweet, impossible memories
Jews used to buy themselves in America.

The two of them beamed,
Gold-toothed, as if their exile were cancelled.
You should eat and be healthy, they said.

Two Relatives

1. The Clown, My Uncle Moishe, Always

Upset the Chinese Checker board when losing;
Made jello for me; gave me a green glass necklace.
He kept the Bronx apartment opulent
Against the grisly wind beyond the pane.

2. Aunt Lena's Hair

My old Aunt Lena
Undid her steelgrey braid
And the hair came tumbling—
River, recall your source.

Sonnet. To Tell the Truth

To tell the truth, those brick Housing Authority buildings
For whose loveliness no soul had planned,
Like random dominoes stood, worn out and facing each other,
Creating the enclosure that was our home.

Long basement corridors connected one house to another
And had a special smell, from old bicycles and baby carriages
In the storage rooms. The elevators
Were used by kissing teenagers.

The playground—iron swingchains, fences, iron monkey bars,
Iron seesaw handles, doubtless now rusted—
Left a strong iron smell on my hands and in the autumn air
And rang with cries. To me it is even precious

Where they chased the local Mongoloid, yelling "Stupid Joey!
                                                             Stupid Joey!"
Now I've said everything nice I can about this.

As Forests Dead and Resting

As forests dead and resting become coal, and then as coal
Contracts, clarifies and becomes diamond, all
My childhood's summer nights have changed
To one night, clear as glass.

That evening sun is behind a row of rosy
Houses along First Avenue, traffic is honking, the sky
Grows fiery, grows amber. Humid heat
Still overhangs New York, like a sick, wicked cat.
People are caught under its bellyfur, panting.
I watch them mass outside, to sit on the benches,
To get the air. Somebody turns
A johnny pump on in the Project parkinglot.
Children wade and float in their inner tubes.
The big ones have wet battles.
Two boys rush toward the hydrant's mouth, to be
Thrown from their feet by the torrent, and bright water
Glistens and flies from them. It is getting darker.

In the full dark, everyone gathers under
Floodlights and songs that stream from a tall building
Into a steelwire pale, as thick as leaves
In autumn woods. Girls laugh. Old men and old
Ladies put away beer. My mother is talking
To a neighbor. *Besame mucho*
Sings Mario Lanza, everyone starts
To dance, the victrola rasps, and my father
Has his arms around me. We are doing his quick foxtrot.

And then the grownups have left. It is very late.
It is moist and cool as leafmold.
A long, complicated game of ringaleevio
Goes on in the lamplit street,
Calls rise like fragments of fire. I call goodnight.

Old Men

It seems to me the kindliness of old men
Is something incommunicably vast.
My grandfather, behind them all, plays chess
With learned Yiddish Socialists in Heaven,
Where he awaits me slipping onto his knee
To hear "The Story of the Man Who Travelled
From Place to Place." My other grandfather,
Who sat in a brown chair near the piano,
Not permitted by his wife to talk,
But smiling shyly, like a house aflame,
Waits also. And an Irishman named Frank,
Who trimmed the bushes in the Project gardens,
Called me "Margaret O'Brien" for my braids,
And let me use the shears. Lastly my dad's friends
Who lived like sheep in lonely East Side playgrounds,
Petted me, taught me checkers patiently,
For many windy autumns.
It seems to me then God's a grandfather;
Infinite tenderness, infinite distance—
Not that I have any religion, but
It seems the way to talk about old men.

Clothing and Nothing
What is it like for us?
Kate Ellis

Friend, it's like this—clothes and the girl I sing,
And a neighborhood where girls had Communion dresses
Lacy as lilies, they had Easter outfits
Pastel and proud, I thought they were angels.
In school they had cashmeres from Saks. But as
For me, my mother's cousins dropped my clothing
Like helicopter pamphlets. It was loose.
It flapped as if it wanted somebody else.
This made me feel like nothing.

At night a princess, I went to visit my peasants,
Wrapped in my bedspread, incognito, silver
And gold in hand to give the loyal ones.
They loved me then. My other role was Wonder
Woman, incredibly speedy, athletic, good-hearted,
My bathing suit the same
Colors as the flag, and skin-tight.
I checked myself in mirrors. You would never dream
Nothing was there. But I knew it.

I am grown up. I have read Dostoevsky,
Kafka and Kierkegaard.
Now I know all about nothing—

Have learned we share this hollow. Friend, we need
A coloration, something fine, some pretty
Clothing, or faith, to make us feel like something.

Annie, Aphrodite and the Elevator

Annie was some years older, so I trusted,
As still I would, her wisdom.
She went to Sacred Heart, where the nuns beat you,
But wore that shield, pierceless gentility,
And blond fluctuating hair.

She had this freckled brother, and one winter
Intriguing weeks went by, until at last
The long-expected messages wafted
As if on wings—He wants to be your boyfriend—
He wants to kiss you.
I said: "I'll ask my mother."
My mother's reply, so ambiguous I couldn't understand a word,
Concluded: "Use your judgment."

I used my judgment in the elevator.
We were ladylike—Annie and me—in the elevator,
Ardently resisting, then submitting,
Like in the movies. Tommy's face came close,
Filled the horizon, and I shut my eyes.
We pushed our lips together, hard as we could, as hard as nails,
As hard as porcelain shepherdess and shepherd.
To me he smelled rusty, like an old frying pan.
But Annie and her boyfriend were truly in love.
She'd said: "He's such a gentleman,"
"I'd like to give myself," and "He respects me."
I could easily see they did it the right way,
And how sustained and wonderful that was,
As we rode to Five in the elevator.
Numerous times we ascended and descended.
That was the winter's tale,

And it was springtime when they finished the walkway
Over the East River Drive... we wanted to try it.
The bridge was empty, except for a man in brown
Who seemed to glance at us, wrote something
On the railing, then sauntered down the ramp, toward the river.
He certainly looked bad, so we rushed over. It said:
FUCK YOU IN YOUR HOT RED JUICY BLOODY CUNTS
—And a phone number. We breathed, giggled, and fled.
Waveblossom, laughing girl, we never discussed
The theme of maidenhead.

The Little Friend

Now last summer of together
(I was twelve and moving)
A scorcher day I asked my friend
Annie did she want
To go to the pool.

She said: "No." I said: "Why not?"
She said: "I have the curse.

Was this some Catholic thing? She
Could see I didn't get it.

"You know, I have a friend visiting," she smiled.
I said (hurt): "What friend?"
She said (looking
Ever so pretty and a little coy):
"A little *red* friend".

All I had known was the book word for that.
It was less picturesque.

Then she chuckled at me
(Blond hair like breeze, blue eyes like sea)
To tell me I had still to learn a lot.

Per Aspera Ad Astra
or
Education Sentimental of a Stubborn Adolescent

> *It's been suggested that atoms in your body have been ... ejected many times ... from exploding stars.*
>
> J.P. Ostriker

Sometimes things work.
I remember my rich friend Susan,
A busty girl, her papa the art dealer,
And her *maman*, the French tiara and oily
Afternoon massage, all generously drawing
In tow the stubborn adolescent—
This was just off Fifth Avenue, very nice,
Many baroque details.
Although to opera, to theater, and especially
To gourmet suppers cooked by Dora or Cora
I'd proved impervious, they
Kept on trying.
I was their little diamond, they would stroke
The crusty Brooklyn off me.

What worked, it happens, was a Van Gogh show
Opening at the Metropolitan
One winter evening. Though cold, though ungrateful,
Wandering confused among the odorous fur coats
I half wanted to stab, and half to lick
With my tongue, what was the painting I gazed at
And suddenly fell like a stone to the knees of my mind?
Was it *The Starry Night?*
Vision in which—and my man the astronomer
Now promises that this is perfect fact—
The galaxies so fill our universe
No space is empty of divinity?
Yes, I was born. Somehow
One does it, coming clean, again exploding.

Love & Food

I fell in love with a doll.
O and a dish.
Although the cynosure of eyes
At the Young Men's & Women's Hebrew Association,
Tall, dark, and two years older—oh please—I attempt—
Kindly he shone gruff me, and asked me out.
Might have been sitting in mountain daisy cloud.
His jokes anent the chowmein I thought heavenly.

In Printing Trades High School was he,
The Union then like his beerdrink Pop,
And his manner was the manner of the real world,
Not like those Fieldston boys,
None of whom, and I felt this was a record,
Ever wanted to date me in six whole years.
Even though I got on the literary magazine
I mostly shunned student activity.

His smile above all I remember.
Lying ecstatic in virginal bed, I imagined his body was stars
(Later read Juliet's aria, the same)
Our first kiss, we sat in the stairwell for,
Took a gradual hour to happen, and lasted always.

Many, than Lee Choy's, properer afterwards,
Hot beef in the Szechuan, in Chen's the Peking Duck.
But shall I praise
His grace, his tenderness?
In '52, we watched Stevenson lose.
For years, until I went to college,
We made out in his forest green enamel'd Chevrolet,
And at Orchard Beach, anointed in hot light, a chocolate cone
He bought me. Thank you, Eddie, for I was hungry.

Communitas

For Simon Linnick, my grandfather, d. 1945

In front of my grandmother's house, I throw my Spalding
Against the wall, and catch it with a sigh,
Oh grandfather, and the hot April sun shining
On me who will never die, will never die.

*

To see, for the first time, one's fabled father
Helpless in the open mouth of pain
Was what he told, or taught, not looking, when he asked,
"Alicia, guess whose funeral Momiss and I
Went to recently." It seemed a funny question
As we were coming from the El to grandma's
House, a winter noon,
He in his frayed jacket, I in my snowsuit.
I watched my black boots walking the puddled pavement,
The snowball bushes pass in these Brooklyn gardens.
"Roosevelt?" I hazarded, knowing this was wrong.
"No, guess again," he said. I cannot remember
Everything that passed before he whispered
The thing he'd wanted me to say, to know
Myself, and I'd refused.
So I saw him surrender, white, to pain,
Curled like a morsel on its steaming tongue,
Whispering "It was your grandpa"—
As I became the mother of my father,
As hot tears fell, as I walked on and on.

*

Inside the house, they drank hot tea, in long
Sugary glasses, after my grandfather
Died, as well as before. The translucent curtains
Drifted, gently. I sat drawing beautiful girls.

*

Simon, that was your name, you gentle Jewish
Atheist, socialist, chess-player. I have no children
Named after you. My father, David,
Is also dead. Your wife Anna, long in the Workman's Circle
Home for the Aged, some of those years with another husband,
Is said to be a hundred years old. Sitting in her gleaming wheelchair,
The brace on her leg, she wants us all to kiss her
Many many times, she raises her evaporating
Bird's cheek, to our lips. It is sweet to kiss her, as to breathe
Flowers, although she is odorless. Your daughter, Beatrice,
Widowed, falls in love like a teenaged girl,
Urgently multiplying the living cells throughout her body.
You were my first death, Simon.
In third grade, the little girl, myself, stood in line longing
For you; carrying you, like a changing silver moon
In her heart. None knew
The pain. At night, sitting in bed, hearing a roaring wind,
She repeatedly said: Dear God, in case you exist, please
Let my grandfather into heaven, even though he didn't
Believe in you, because he was a good man.
Simon, I don't even know where you're buried, you must
Inhabit one of those vast cities of grey-white stone
Outstretched in dignity and peace, in Brooklyn.
I am sure you have forgotten your shabby pharmacy,
Your kisses of smooth-voiced Anna, to whom you wrote Yiddish
Letters, and your intellectual youth, when through
The Russian underground you burrowed westward toward liberty.
It is a long way from Russia. My husband, I swear it,
Is a good man, with bright bewildered eyes. Here,
Here is my hand, Simon. Our children
Show us their heels. It is ages
Since I have spoken with you.

*

"We measure this by that, we come to see,
We touch what's close; for what is far, we yearn;
Mankind must then make one community."
This is as true as that the dead return.

*

From the box, one gem more, and I'm through.
In this proposition, you hug me on your lap,
But I am shouting and angry,
But you insist that you refuse to vote,
Because no President will save the Jews
In Europe. Hold me. Don't cry.
Kind canker on my budding patriotism, your lip
Nuzzles my cheek. You tickle me. My throat
Hurts with its trust of you.

II

A threefold cord is not easily broken.
                                    Ecclesiastes

Portraite D'Artiste

When everybody's in bed
And you are away,
I'm alone, working on woodcuts,
Accompanied by a radio.
I print, revise, print,
I lay the ricepaper in rows on shelves.
I am trying, in this print,
To represent, simultaneously,
Two smoothed stones, such as one finds by the ocean;
Fruit—a pear for example;
And a torso, divided by a backbone and containing
A curled foetus. The colors
Are grays and pink oranges. I try also
To retain the wood grain.
The night is cold.
Meanwhile the hands on my watch
Go around and around.
Later I draw myself, with the baby inside me,
Standing in a long mirror,
Portraite d'artiste enceinte,
Ugly, proud, dignified,
Good bones after all,
Peaceful.

I think, "I was born lonely. I am best so."
And an artist at work can always
Be accompanied by death, which is happy.
But after all,
Most of my nights I spend with your hot body,
First fucking, then curled up together,
Then rolling around back to back and ass to ass,
Which, we have decided, or discovered, is best for sleeping
The whole night through—
I think my mother and father
Slept the same way, if
I remember correctly—
Even in sleep, not separated.

Portrait of a Man

You wear glasses.
You wear blue flannel pajamas.
You are doing calculations on an envelope; and as you pause to think,
The lamp shines on your hands.
Here is your work, that you love
With a mad, faunlike, hidden mind,
Inherited from Pythagoras,
From Al-Jabr, from Descartes, from God knows who.
Very well.
Your profile, toward me, is not
Smooth as in boyhood.
Very well.
Our heating system hums and rattles
Against the November weather
That presses chillingly up
From our backyard at the windowglass.
Some Ravel piano piece storms on the radio
Filling the room with intangible turbulences.
Like nested birds, our children sleep upstairs,
Not yet formed, but forming, becoming strangers.
Very well.
As for me, man, I'm watching your loneliness.
Making a portrait of you.

Of you, who do not wish
To think of the winter approaching
With its wet black wings.

The light outlines
Serviceably the bumps
And indentations of your face and hands.
You rub your blackhaired chest, under the pajamas.
Why this invisible dance? This faithful striving for clarity?
Will our scratches, in fact, correspond to the starry whirl?
Ravel elaborates his terms of climax.
Having cogitated, you begin again to write.

The Wolves

You were clearly pleased with yourselves
For having invented the wolves
I had to lug out from under
Your innocent beds, dear daughters,
Every morning, every damn morning
While that particular
Joke lasted, mommy crouching
To haul the heavy beasts out
By their bushy tails, hoist them and bear
On my back, out the door, down the stairs,
Out the front door, off the balcony
Five flights high—while in your nighties
Of small cotton, pink and pink,
You dreaded the fur and flank—
Each day, heaved them over the railing
And hurried back, shivering.
I did this for your sake;
You held your fright like a cup.
You dreamed them, and I had to break
Their necks, before you'd get up.

Fire: A Parable

All that I feared occurred.
The music made a fire, that was
Infants burning to ashes in the sunrise
More and more quickly, and that was
All right, clean comedy, I perceived this
And you made a fire and I carefully crawled into it
Closer, purple rimmed yet increasingly invisible white-
Flare interior, approached, so easily, pierced in, drumming
Toward the smile, for yes, all terror, a flaming serpent, circled
Smiling, my words floated like bubbles to you, companion, petal
After petal fell, forgetful, from the chrysanthemum, almost I
Disappeared, or grew transparent, opening, until the center,
Where it lay, of which the function is to mutter
Don't touch me, don't touch me,
Don't touch me ever! O send washing waves—
No use, it does not melt, it does not break—
It is hardness, blackness, anger, separation,
Stupidity. So we made love, love,
Stonelike. Selfhood is a stone.

Cape Hatteras, Easter Weekend

i

Weathered wood:
No people:
Seashells:
Wind:
Sand:
Grass:
A straight highway,
A bleached hand.

ii

The child sings:
I don't want to fall, fall, fall,
Into the water, water.
But I can't fall into the water,
Because I am on a bridge.

iii

In fishing towns here on Cape Hatteras
Roads go grassy
At dead ends, boats nod on the water.
Nets, tackle;
How far we are from home.
Both the flowerbeds in the gardens
And the perimeters of graves
Are marked with conches.

iv

I don't know, I don't know,
I don't know, I don't know,
Sings the smaller daughter to the tune
Of Twinkle Twinkle Little Star.
Her legs don't like to hike.
Wind hurts her eyes.

But when we reach the lighthouse
That seems to walk the water,
She stamps her feet.
I'm climbing up! I'm climbing up! she cries.

v

On the sand the black carcass
Of a six-foot porpoise that has been shot
By somebody from the nearby Air Force Base
Dries in wind.
The sun is for this.
And the etched seashells,
Embedded here like stars, are not yet wasted,
Although their animals have been eaten
Or have become sand.

Our own footsteps
Come up from the tide
And the slight footsteps of our children
Over sand mountains.

vi

You ran with me
Along some sand.
The beach seemed endless
And the sea was shining.

The stars were numberless.
Have, love, keep.
Don't cry in your mind.
Don't fall asleep.

vii

I walk by the row of tents and trailers
With a load of diapers to wash.
It is middle morning, cold, sunny and clear.
Families are cleaning up.
Men ready fishing gear.
Looking up, I see kites in the sky.
On a table the dishwashing liquid
Phallus-shaped bottle reads *JOY.*

The Hills

Twilight goes down to darkness.
We are driving, and the black
Houses on rocky hills,
Those human grief shapes,
Or hope shells, each send up
Thin smoke, that the long lip
Of a grey sky drinks from.

Their chimneys jut, home,
Home, home, as we drive by,
Talking quietly, our children
Hungry and sleepy, wrapped in
Their blankets. A river travels beside us,
And seems to be trying to speak. We imagine
The decent lives, the clean rooms,

Tables, beds, dusty cupboards,
Clocks, changes happening anyway,
As we drive to our own place.

Skating

The moon and all the stars
Watch over us as we
Skate over the frozen lake
Smoothly and slowly.

The oaks and beeches are
Making one dark orbit.
There are lights from houses.
The ice is gray, gray, gray is it.

In all the silence is
The hiss of our blades making
Their crisp tracks, and at times
Deep ice, abruptly, barking.

Property

We drive a mile up a dirt road, green shadows
And rocks swallowing the car.
Then a big birch bursts white, in sunlight, framing the driveway.
We emerge with our suitcases, sleeping bags, boxes of food.
We stretch our muscles.

My husband and girls disappear down the path to the pond.
Sweating, getting ready for a swim myself,
I put things away in our little cabin, built
By an old man's hands when his wife died.
He left the town below, lived here alone
Ten summers and winters with his dog and chickens.
Sometimes I touch his ragged ghost.

Beside the path, the trees start. Weedy poplars
Skirt the edges, like majorettes.
Going through, swinging a scythe to clear the trails,
I have seen the old stone walls, fallen and mossy,
Records of human failure against stone—
Days when they tried to farm New England—
And there's an abandoned quartz quarry, hidden and dangerous,
Another old summoner of men's lives,
And then the beech, oak, fir, deep in the woods,
Not huge but growing, a second growth,
An army deciding what to do next, reassembling
Its forces. I want to protect it.

Buying land was like getting married, like having babies,
A dumb commitment to love, to time, my husband's eyes,
His hands, or a pond and meadow, a trail through beeches,
A ramshackle cabin. Wanting it, even not knowing it,
Even believing "This is my property."

Now I am ready to swim, I collect my towel,
I am hot and happy in this Berkshire afternoon.
We visit, but nothing pays any attention to us.
We listen to birds, insects, wind, frogs in evening,
And the flow of the icy stream across the road.
We would gladly hear the noise of things growing.
The land takes care of itself, progresses
Like a busy wife whispering messages to herself
As she cooks, cleans, mends, and raises her children.

The Incompleat Gardener

The sun's burned through the fog, the weather is nice and sexy.
But in the cabin, we're overwhelmed by a swamp of garbage smell,
Garbage smell, garbage smell everywhere, ugh, on account of Bienens
Visit, adorers of good food, get way too much, can't even stuff it on shelves,
Cook some, it's marvelous, two days we gorge ourselves, then goodbye
Parents and kiddies all, leaving us swill and garbage smell

Hello Bienens, now you're immortal

But that's not what I want to tell
For the girls call me MOMMY AN ANIMALS IN THE GARDEN
And it's true! Ravished! Woe!
My little tepid garden, that hopefully despite my unlucky black thumb I planted,
And it's not my fault, I'm a city girl, what do I know—
Planted, and put down lime and some fertilizer, put chicken wire around,
Watered every dry morning at just about dawn after Gabriel woke me
And I put some Cheerios in a bowl in his crib for him
Got a bucket and a watering canful, *twiceover,* from the stream—
After watering can empty put bucketwater in it, then halfbucket left,
Pour that too, then the whole thing over was enough, virtuous yes but
I loved them too, my poor skimpy two rows of carrots and a new row coming up,
Two rows of lettuce at last squeezing along there, a row of radishes,
And an L of third generation tomatoes (first two generations et)
That I myself had experienced the drooping of, transplanted, and had urged along—
Sometimes even feeling and hearing them grow—
Even before this, it was depressing enough.
Why can't my garden be like Paul's?
    Come into my garden and taste the pleasant fruits,
      yeah man,
A jungle out of sight! Come into my garden and taste my pleasant fruits!
Lettuces, I'm telling you, a row of crisp fat petticoated houris!
Impenetrable unthinned carrot wall!
Gross-leaved kohl rabi! heavy erotic politburo tomatoes! green corn rising!
Peas, of undreamt-of delicacy! Deific purple cabbages! Everything sumptuous!

Ah Paul,
      success is counted sweetest by those who ne'er succeed,
      to comprehend a nectar requires sorest need
                              I told you Sunday—
Well, he had a horse, that's why.
But what about Hattie Greenberg's garden up the road?
I snuck in one day to look and came back so blue...
She has a mulch pile, that's why. And it doesn't smell after all. We'll
                                          start one too.
But even so, pathetic as my plants were, I did feel something for them,
Affectionate, which can't be helped, and hopeful, which springs eternal,
Looking forward pridefully to eating the poor things—
But now! What! All my pretty ones?
Could he not spare
Ah curses on you you rotten raccoon or woodchuck or whatever you are
Screw you! It's not fair!

Jerry next morn go down get milk for breakfast
On account of our milk rotten no wonder after 3 days in stream—
Another Bienen responsibility you remember them—
Ask Carl what do about varmints Carl say dried blood good only for rabbits;
Is your fence six foot high? other possibilities = poison bait,
Or — he doesn't say "shoot" but makes thumbforefinger gesture — tactfully —
Or — set trap, catch critter, put in car, drive ten miles away & release
Or — have a dog.
He own traps, but has lent them to somebody.

On my way to stream, see treetoad, just where cross log.
Admire nice brown color, markings.
But he becomes aware of me and with a terrible shiver squeezes himself under
                                          the log.

                                          for Paul Metcalf, neighbor

Wine

Going to drink the wine, I find a yellowjacket in it.
The yellowjacket I get out with a bit of paper towel, still alive.
The wine I'll use for stew.

Down at the pond. The girls have brought a carton full
Of towels, bathing suits, fig bars, peanuts. Their hair
Is loose. They run in the meadow, naked.

>   Is this the way, trying this tentative
>   Expansiveness, as Eve and Rebecca run gaily
>   Forward? Is the soil rich and poisonless?

On house in town, fresh paint, a spritely white. Even in
This depressed area, where boys can choose the Army or
Welfare.

The young fry among the goldfish swim in clusters, rather
Gawky and random. They break the water surface frequently,
Making little glitters—for they are snapping at every speck—
Food or not, and eager to taste the alien element, whereas
The older, golder, goldfish, swim in groups, leisurely and
Graceful without waste effort, they like to hover
Motionless near the surface in the sun.

The mouse or mice is very bold. Seen him scuttle in daylight,
Not only up the chimney outside, but in the cabin. Last night
He woke us with great noise, and in the morning we found he'd
Been trying to drag a pacifier out through his hole; this
Seems ominous.

>   J. holds the baby, who has been crying
>   Love/ a fountain
>   Fast as you pull them up, the weeds grow wild

But the garden is better this summer. We'll have tomatoes
In abundance, squash, carrots, we'll hold our heads up, we'll
Invite everyone, we'll drink a lot of wine.

The Killing

> *Neither shall they learn war any more.*
> Isaiah

The killing will not stop. A scarlet
Hail is always behind my eyes.
The morning paper, shreds of flesh,
Poisons the bread, the salt, the cheese.

Husband, I want to fight the good
Battle of hip, and breast, and thigh,
Where pleasure, spoil of sinew, breeds
Outrageous generosity—

I want to see our children spring
Free as this coarse grass. I suppose
The killing will not stop, the killing
Will not stop. Who knows. Who knows.

III

Speech after long silence. It is right,
All other friends being estranged or dead...
That we descant, and yet again descant
Upon the supreme theme of Art and Song.
            W.B. Yeats

The Fool Stands up to Teach King Lear Again

in memory of Paul Goodman

The systematic murder of the young
Before they reach me, by stupid and crippled elders,
The bland, blank-faced rejection of their own
Depths, by the secret terror that nails them
To hold very still, praying not to be seen
By the teacher, each other, themselves—
Baffles me. *Ripeness is all.* I think of those classroom walls
Painted quite to resemble stale vomit.
There they sit; and among them the still
Intelligent and eager, the green fruit
That well may rot before we ripen it.

Furthermore: consider my incompetence, my laziness, my
Inability to tell jokes. Why
Should anybody listen? O failure! failure!
My stomach flutters and jams, I am terrified
Of knowing nothing, except that beauty is truth—
Useless, and the wrong poet. Then once more,
None does offend—none! I say none! I'll able 'em,
Yells the mad king, who ables us. *Come, boy,*
I rush in late, open the book, stand there:
All I can do is demonstrate my joy.

Noon Concert

It is something like water drops, and it is something
Like a weaving you might make to offer a friend
Who visits from another state
                          Kyrie eleison
       the consort has been
       walking in the museum courtyard
       by the pool and sculptures
                in their medieval dress
                some of the girls were dancing on the grass
                some of the boys were joking
                                Sanctus
                                Domine

—Only who are we, seated rapturously together,
Each secretly hungering and thirsting
       for the rain, for the divine rain
       believing that it must fall sweetly, strongly—
           do we make
           a community of the needy
           seated on the warm stone floor?

    A group of children up front with their teachers.
On the Gothic balcony a man with lilacs
    leans with his man-friend.
                          Gloomy, the crucifixions
                          hang on the walls, and the singers and players
                          develop the offertorium to march us
                          from hell's jaws upward into holy light

                                Agnus dei
                                Qui tollis peccata mundi
                                The little drums, the voices,
                                    a gentle thunder

                    Partly a matter of the music
                    half a millenium old
                         partly a matter of our common thirst—
     Fool, from the parched tongue's self springs the full fountain—
And so they sing, freely.

            Busch-Reisinger Museum, Cambridge, Massachusetts

The Clock Above the Kitchen Door Says One

*The devil is, if you write an excellent poem
I am glad, you know, but when your sullen, milky
Tongue hung, last year, following me, I drank...
Needed. Come back.* — The new dull waitress comes
Out of the kitchen, sets down soup, salad,
Hamburgers, beers, she is feeding the academics,
Her lipstick smeared, on the checkered tablecloth.
She lacks the cockney temper of Doris, who quit.
We lack the music mankind yearns asleep for.

The devil is, I want you to love me
Here in the Corner Tavern, while I tell you
About Poetry. — We wipe our mouths with paper napkins,
We're spitting blood, we're coughing, we're killing time,
We're eating lunch. Keats was dead when he was your age,
When he was my age, Mozart.

In the Museum

A true artist always leaves something muddy
In order not to confuse himself with his imitators
           the paint shows/ raw mud/ clay
                                          toe
        tracks
              Cézanne—the verticals (poplars) simply contend
           against the tilted (hillside) plane markt in rectangular
      fields and both foliage clumps and rectangular
    rooftops balance these   plus a canal
            I didn't first notice but which
            is the largest single color area
                gray—hidden at the bottom of the hills it
                  is only in the middle of the
                            painting but alone flows/ *MUST* flow
                                  out of it
                                  the painting

A flick, Cezanne, like a venetian blind
There is a kind of hidden and discreet quality
in a Cezanne painting always?
        Tactile like a card shark
            laying his flat rectangles on the wood?

The plump matrons in the museum
      all made of tender flesh
      all put together
                  and chattering happily and reverently
   must, of course, be the artworks themselves
                                in their hats
              (this ain't my novel thought)
       Look at Vuillard reach out of his painting
               and grab a matron with her flushy colors!

I personally like the sound of feet on museum floors
    clicking and echoing
        and would cheerfully lick and eat this sound
                      like a vanilla ice cream cone

    —like the matrons stepping and whispering
                    reverently
              in their tailored suits
          the generously endowed matrons
        in the generously endowed museum
                    to whom I am being unkind
                      (not really)
  money is soft like flush like flesh is soft
  in their lovesome hats

    but marble's hard and lofty
        a balance between these is what's required
        is had, here
        that's why I'm happy
                    I am happy because
we know those painters painted with their pricks
the matrons, unaware
they feel it
these galleries of supple pricks smiling on them
and arousing them

arousing in them an exhilaration
they too wish to be artists immediately
and they are, a little bit
that's why they're happy

I am happy because they are happy
confronted by galleries of supple smiling pricks
that radiate the glory of heavens upon us, we
must, we must become artists

like once in the Metropolitan suddenly I heard
blotting everything out, or fusing with everything
the Blake line in my head
in that furnished spaciousness—the Blake line

      "And Milton said, What do I here without my emanation?"
meaning—
      "And Milton said, What do I here without my emanation?"
meaning—
          a rectangle, a cone, a sphere
        this struck, and struck again
        oars in a stream.

The Colleague

<blockquote>after reading William Carlos Williams, Early Poems</blockquote>

Gray face, it does no good,
Even if I met you, to agree
That it's nothing, all of it,
Vacuo, *NADA,* emptihood, space, where we
Expected pith; or evil, slime
At root and blossom and fruit,
Polluted, filthy waters, slippery and grimy
Air and pavement, horrible hoot
Of horns and drums, we might
As well make love rather
Than agree about it, whatever
We would agree on, brother,
Don't you think, gripping
A fleshly rhetoric, it would
Be worth one's while to rip
The bedclothes from the bed,
To hear the swooning tide
That drowns the dirty sheets,
And make the mattress sweat
And creak, at last, at last
Toward oblivion! So frail
This frame is, bones brittle as eggshells,
Breakable as a blonde child
Wiping her nose on her sleeve that we might
As well do that, don't
You think, don't you suppose, and hasten
To our old ways again, you to your grave,
Rectified, I to my life.

Thirst

after a Departmental Luncheon

Christ damn these drunken lunches I go to, where all
Are my strangers, and I am a fool—and my shyness and shackles—
Mankind, this puke—and the voice reminding me I don't care,
When I might touch you, find you, or you, anyone, your hair,
Your tongue for my tongue, that would be real, or read poems, and burst
Into tears from the words of the true justices, toward my true thirst.

My Lecture to the Writing Students

Alive, alive, the poem has to be alive.
It doesn't have to be correct, kids.
If it's alive, the correctness will take care of itself.

I feel like chewing the wine today.
I continue, inspired: the poem
Is insane, it wants

To tie tin cans to its tail
To fly away with General Motors under one arm
The Sacred Heart under the other, it wants

To express the fluid explosion in your mind
The subjective,
Transient, and not verbal

(the smell like an orange
how you feel about your father)

In a form objective, permanent
And verbal. O cuckoo! The right
Words, in the right order—

Isn't that hard enough?
Isn't it impossible enough
Ever to strike the full, accurate chord?

And you want to interfere
With that task
By writing Poetry?

(a la Wallace Stevens?)
Haven't you realized yet that the Masters
Were horses—whipped,

I say whipped, by realities
That needed to get to an inn
By midnight? that needed

A willing horse
To
Draw them where they were going?

New Jersey Sunset

The corner. Eats, eats, more eats.
BLIMPIE BASE AN ADVENTURE IN KARENS & KAROLS FROZE CUSTARD DELICAT ESSEN
                string matchbook butts a straw
                                  gum wrappers on

                                    in art,
                          one does not loathe
                          what is loathsome

                    *

Damned hot, hot
Although the morning was cool.
Heat like a zoo.
A cop directs the fuming traffic, a crowd
Is waiting for the bus I'm waiting for
Sweating. I'm all eyes, I like
Especially the hostile, the insolent, the flashy
Ebony chicks with purple pants or swinging it
Heavy long legs wooly wild heads in pride
And meek young nurses   Studying their first flesh
Liberty, make
That tree bloom, sister, go ahead push it out (rainbows
From this balance spring) legs feel so caressed
In stockings, hides the freckles or the hair
Or whatever maladjustments the skin itself—
Life, whatever—
And the middle class and more
Than middle aged ladies in house dresses
And shoes killing the time of day, each bearing
More than wrinkled shopping bags
Stuffed with the sins of men, O weary reck'ning

>Aha, the purple pants
>has dropped some garbage on the street, with scorn
>(already much littered)
>—But she does it to prove
>(but not yet is she liberated)

Delicious human smash, like stirring a viscous fluid

>*HERE COMES THE BUS*
>*HERE COMES THE BUS*

Into the bus
>Paranoid driver

Slumped in the bitter grays of long service
Grudges our passage, sends out the deathrays, hurls over change
I follow rump of youth, goodbye to street

>*

Inside the bus
>kind of empty back

Little kids jiving each other
And the sleepy grownups look the other way.

>Boy sits
>with a green balloon
>wagging it idly
>up & down, up & down
>slips
>>somebody else retrieves
>
>he sits
>little pants
>on his mama's lap

>>Student reads
>>*HUNGARY IN THE LATE NINETEENTH*
>>(Chapter V The Peasantry)
>>dressed in black
>>pen in pocket

       sighing, too thin
       too thin the book folder
       his shoulders, his thighs, his watch
       that goes around
       and around
       (Chapter V The Peasantry)

            Man gazes
            at row of public service posters
            "Pot" "Ups" "Downs" "Acid" "Smack" (photographs
            in living color on an electric blue ground)
            and the legend "Why Do You Think They Call It Dope?"
            he hugs his paper bag, he blinks old eyes

                IN ART   REMEMBER   IN ART
                                           (inert
              everybody is a pocket) hey
              shove forthing on young studs in freaky dress
              embracing selfy silk mid eyes of glue
              to unappreciating world
              and sticky crowd coagulant alive
                    as odors rise
                        STEP TO THE REAR OF THE BUS
                        STEP TO THE REAR OF THE BUS
              nobody does
Up front our driver curses in the heat
And hates the people and his sweaty feet

I can love him & him & you & you
The bus bangs forwards, showing how to do.

The sun is setting. Whatever
Is outside, on Rte. 27, goes swiftly by.

IV

*Spring One. Spring One. I am Eagle. I am Eagle.
I can hear you very well. I feel excellent.
My feeling is excellent.*

> Major Gherman Titov, aboard Soviet spaceship
> Vostok II, August 7, 1961.

A Dream of Springtime

Three boys working
on an old Buick:
their hands grow darker and greasier.

*

As the tongue plunges, as the rose receives

        The specific fragrance on the bee's body tells
           what kind of flower to hunt
                      in the round dance
        with increasing distance between the feeding place
        and the hive, the number of straight runs
        within the waggle dance decreases

*

The president
the present
the president declares
                Don't you touch me or I'll go *crazy*

(Everybody get together now and picture gibbering President
        like, see, his whole jaw is wobbling like Jello
        & he's got a straitjacket on but his body is trembling
        violently, like a eucalyptus leaf, & his pathetic doggy
        eyes are filled with tears of rage, he's in
        this padded cell, see, & making screeching retarded
        hospital noises   hnnnh! hnnnh! hnnnh!
                                                  —drools)

        plutonium reacting half-mile under
        won't kill the cactus or the running lizard
        yet
                When the dawn Times sings Portugese in African
                colonies lately are raping the prisoners' wives

High though ignorant, their hair fabulous
Their legs vibrating and their heads going Wheeeee—

*

It is quite clear that the person on whose behalf I have promised
To write a letter to certain authorities inquiring after
The causes and conditions of his imprisonment, which
Happens to be political imprisonment, having been
Told that the only thing which may save these people
Is outside pressure, and have neither written
Any letters nor now can find my piece of paper
With the information and the name from the list that
Was checked off and given to me: quite clear that this
Person, a young engineering student who has been in
Jail for x years of a y-year sentence will stay
There because I had his name and have not written.
I'm no worse than anybody else.

*

Thunderstorms tumble, the largest natural sound, could be surf
Waterfall cascades
Against small nature sounds: night ones: a long cricket or frog trrr
And trill trill, here comes dawn, sky whitens, birds arise

Then the quick piano creates a smoky room.

*

They turn over in their sleeping bags,
Three forms side by side in the bed
Of needles, not using a tent.
The three sequoia vaulted above their heads
Have been exhaling mildly since twilight.
Dew is collecting
              and this demureness,
                 this air, the birth-sweet loveliness
                    that they are sleeping through
         will be gone
         by the time the sun is up, but
           for now the coolness caresses their white cheeks.

        then slaying them before their eyes
        and pulling out their nails and making
        them eat "portions of their bodies"
        everybody knows what portions
        everybody grins
        everybody knows there is nothing new
        every human being at the bottom of a soundless
             dream, a nightmare, deeper than tides, than light's reach
             deeper than milk, where the one
             being gropes to collect its immortal flesh
             that flesh composed of all brothers and sisters
             cries, Lord, what do I do
             to make these fragments whole and beautiful
                  and at the middle level of this dream
                  every human being craves to become the torturer
                  every human being craves to become the victim
        buoyant, we waken
        and the president declares:
        Don't come near me, now
        don't you dare come near me
        don't you touch me or I'll go *crazy*

                    I swear I'll climb the *walls*

                    ii

Oh joy! I've got an orange California Poppy in my yard
Right in the back by the fence! Always wanted one! Just noticed
It wheeling bike out with Gabriel to go shopping
It's Sunday morning—

California poppies are so great—their
Petals are smooth—skinlike—look easily
Ripped and they're always these fantastic
Nymphet dayglo hot loud colors, so

They're like some kind of girls who are
Young skinny, cigarette lipped, like wear shrunk
Sweaters and just crazy—standing
On corners under moist streetlights at night

*

It may be raining. It's dark.
I have had some coffee and plan to stay up.
Yeah yeah, the weeping Pleiades wester,
Sappho.

*

Somebody is very thoughtfully making love. That's all
I can think of. The sheets are greyed and mussed,
The blankets far gone. The room is immobile and nothing
Much. They have a lot of cigarette butts in the glass
Ashtray. It's like walking up a street
Looking in the storewindows, something always
Mysteriously profound looking back, vaguely glossy, in addition
To the watches, television consoles, silver sequins
Involved in the windowdressing with the rayon
Lace-trimmed slips and the crepe paper strips twisted
Across and down and the perfectly black glazed
Ceramic cheetah in the gift shop window. Certainly
Numerous others belonging to the same
Neighborhood also are walking on this street.
Some are going into the bakery. Some are
Buying the Daily News on the corner and checking
The racing column rapidly. An elevated
Train rattles by like the cavalry once in a while,
With the result that the whole room, with the bed in it,
Rattles responsively though briefly. I must also
Remark that 4 p.m. sunshine is streaming through
The window, though the window is like a small
Dirty boy that has not been washed in quite
Some time. Well, there come the morning birds again.
Every day, they wake up in their nests with the chilly
Air brushing their feathery backs and the unprotected tops
Of their heads, slipping through branches, and they start singing.
The creek, swollen and excited from the melting

Freshets that are trickling into it everywhere,
Like a beautiful woman unafraid is dashing
Over the stones. This is flutes, violins in disguise
As you have probably guessed. The fish are
Delighted and cold, in this divine springtime
Water that is rushing over the permanent rocks.
At the bottom of the hill where the creek crosses the
Road, there is a Shell Oil station on one side and
A shack with a lot of old tires, tin cans, and
Abandoned lumber lying everywhichway nearby.
The lovers have turned over, pulled the
Wrinkled topsheet over their torsos, and fallen
Quite asleep, the bottle of rye whiskey standing
On the end table growing warmer.

He is coughing. He is coughing. He is coughing. He is coughing.

Berkeley, April 1973

Black Men, White Teeth, Berkeley Campus

Expostulating papas so smoothed shaped fired and glazed over
    sheeeeit
they *can't* do anything graceless, they are just music!
  because, see, society is heavy *worked* them
    like the potter the clay smacks toward perfection
so they don't need to do nothing but look for pussy
    even while, ha, they are walking into the Library

      mmmmm-MMM.

    —or the kid last night cutting along the sidewalk
      up in front of us
  toward the Hare Krishna people's drumming
    was swaying his thin butt, shoulderblades
      and raven fingers
  just a little, inflectedly, hm-hm . . . .

        turn around, give me that snowy smile
That beauty, friend, let nothing take away
Let no man conquer, and no nation kill.

The Freeway

> *It is not impossible to conceive the*
> *surprising Liberty that the Americans*
> *enjoy; some idea may likewise be*
> *formed of their extreme equality.*
> De Tocqueville

Flow, riverrun, rapid channel, flow
      over the dancing stones, directly over the
mountainside gravel, directly crushing the fixed protruded
rocks, this is the desert this the desert is, and here
the valley of smokes, the orange trees laid in her lap, and this
the city, nothing is what it is not

You need no longer gaze attentively
nor hunt, emboughed, a fleeting nakedness

As Euclid along the stone lane tracked naked loveliness who shimmered
and vanished forever and forever as he moved, nevertheless believing
"Nothing is what it is not" among blue asphalt silences
like a convoy of motorcycles, just as the sky
the quick   the dead   the race not the swift not
the angels not wetback not lockheed   eat a peach the juices spill
over over over luscious

      honey milk
            vacuous springtime mistress

Easy to mean nothing easy to say easy

Make no mistake the freeway works, like a tube
in a tree, like a rain drop pursuing its stripe down
as fast as it can, which is always faster than, like artery, like
pastel FOREST LAWN billboard mother and child
flowery background peacefully advertising CEMETERY . . .

MORTUARY... EVERYTHING... Everything? Man, at
least everything, like the Kama Sutra, doing it forever, the rhythm
the rhythm the rhythm freedom joy power don't look back
don't look forward either don't look OUT like computer
don't STOP like typewriter like the little engine that could
like Euclid nothing is what it is not, like Coltrane
blowingly insane all freeways are truly One Freeway, the freeway
holiness should become inscribed upon the consciousness of every
automobile owning uebermensch in the US of Amerikay open the
freeway don't be afraid open the freeway don't be afraid open the

PACIFICPACIFICPACIFICPACIFICPACIFICPACIFICPACIFIC